GAME

PLAN

"Wha-t... are you willing to do to grow your business?

Do you have a game plan?"

Necessary strategies to win
at the game of Network Marketing.

By
TONY FLEMING

The Game Plan

Tony Fleming,

Tony Fleming Enterprises

mrtonyfleming@gmail.com

Smyrna, GA 30082

678-644-4541

ISBN: 13: 978-1499733570

ISBN: 10:1499733577

Book Production Provided by

Carriage House Publishing

***The Game Plan** will provide you with the necessary strategies to win at the game of Network Marketing.*

Table of Contents

Another Way

I can remember as if it were yesterday when I first heard a statement that changed my life. When I researched it, I found out that it was a quote from Mr. John D. Rockefeller but it was Mr. J. Paul Getty who made it popular. The statement was, *"I would rather have one percent of 100 people's efforts than 100% of my own."*

I heard this during one of the many training sessions that I attended in my early days in the network marketing industry. That one statement had a great impact on me. To this day, it has kept me going, especially during the ups and downs, while building my business. I always knew I wanted time, I wanted freedom, and I wanted wealth, but I just didn't know where to start.

Back in the day, I had a crew that I hung out with. We all looked and smelled good but none of us had any real money. I knew there was a better way, "another way." I fiercely wanted the "time-freedom-wealth thing" that I had heard so much about and that I knew was out there but I didn't know how to achieve it alone. I had strong ambition and I thank God that there were a number of people that came my way that I could learn from. It was from their training that I formed a Game Plan. I decided to write this book because a few people helped me, and I don't want you to be out there searching. Help is here!

So for those of you who are looking for another way to build wealth, have entered the game of network marketing and don't have a strategy, here is one. . .

THE

GAME

PLAN

The Game Plan

The first thing you MUST do when you get started in business is set up a GAME PLAN MEETING (GPM) with your personal sponsor or someone in your upline. It should be someone who is more knowledgeable in the business and with a track record of success. At this meeting you should talk with your sponsor or upline about your goals and why you've decided to go into business.

If they want you to succeed, they should be willing to do the GPM with you or, at least, connect you to someone in the business who can. I think a person should at least get directions and guidance. It's unfair and irresponsible not to. This is the plan-of-action meeting that they should have with you right at the beginning of your business. It is important! Putting this strategy in place could be the tool you use to reflect on when it gets tough. Unfortunately people quit when it gets tough and business can and will get tough. So they should want to give you ammunition for the fight that is ahead by giving you keys to steer your business in the direction of your goals and dreams. Without that, you have no direction and you may just quit even before you really get started.

That is why I have created this book, just for people like you who are looking for that strategy -that *real* game plan-whether you have someone to sit down with you or not. I want to make sure you have a fighting chance by giving you a plan of action- something in your hands to be able to fight with.

A lot of people who are on my level in the industry don't feel the way that I feel. I started out over 20 years ago trying to build my direct sales business through my experiences and the things I learned; putting the plays together bit by bit, piece by piece. It was hard. With the help of others, I did it. I don't want anyone to have to struggle and fight to understand this business needlessly in the dark. I wrote this book to help as many people as I can to start their business the right way. After you have gotten the basics of the game plan, the rest is up to you.

A lot of times the upline forgets this all important step and they fail to have a GPM, usually because they are so excited to have enrolled you, the brand new business partner, into the business. Unfortunately in this type of business that upline may not see you, but that one time, so they can't afford to forget this step. This is not only their business, this is your business too. To forget it means a setback for them and a slow start for you and your business as well. This happens very often.

Let's suppose, you have no one to help you get started in your business and you have to put your own GPM together, and you only have this book. I'll share with you, six key points that, with practice, you will learn not only how to open each door, but how to skillfully knock those doors down! The only requirement: You will have to be honest with yourself, list your goals and dreams, and admit to yourself how realistic they are.

There are at least six major points that I take the time to go over *every single time* I do a GPM with a new business partner. I want to succeed in business and so should you. In order for us all to really succeed, we must help others. We've all heard, *"What goes around, comes around."* If I take the time to encourage, support and help you to have success, in turn, I do believe in time my rewards will come from the seeds I've planted through this book. It reflects seedtime and harvest plain and simple. Without a GPM, it's virtually impossible for the average person to have success in this industry. That's why I'm taking the time out to write this book. I want you to have success in your business.

When you get started in the business you will have established at least these six things: your why, financial goals, sacrifice, a list of names, categorized your list and your commitment.

After we have gone over these points, I always ask the big question, *"What are you willing to sacrifice to get these six things done?"* I watch the person's body language change as we begin to talk about sacrifice. It's always interesting to watch how people begin to shift and adjust themselves in their seat. They may even look away during the conversation because they are uncomfortable talking about sacrifice. It's just so interesting how the person's body language changes when that particular topic comes up.

If I just happen to have the GPM over the telephone with them, there may be a long pause or they may even start to clear their throat. It never fails! I think at this point in the process they actually realize they are really in a business. And then to ease their tension, because I do understand this is a big pill to swallow if you aren't ready for it, I may start giving examples of different sacrifices that some of my other business partners have made for a certain period of time, but then it's like I'm speaking French. They don't see the need for such a deep sacrifice...at least at first.

I find that most people's goals and

dreams are on a Mercedes Benz level, but their work efforts level is Volkswagen. After a month, six months, or even 12 months there's a falling off, but not before the complaining begins. Most of the time, the answer for why their business hasn't taken off the way they wanted is right there in the mirror.

When I started in the direct sales industry, which some people also call Network Marketing, I gave up a lot because I wanted a lot and I also believed I could win big doing this business. I cut out all TV for two years. Most of my money went back into my business. I traveled and attended all trainings, and, most of all, I did my best to talk to at least five people a day about what I was doing. I was focused. I stayed up late getting organized and worked the phone. In other words, there were serious sacrifices I had to make to become successful and I realized then, over 20 years ago, and I still see it today, that there are a lot of people who aren't willing to pay that price, that is, the price that I paid to reach my goals.

I remember working a corporate sales job years ago. I made a friend at that job named, Curtis Booker. He always won the Salesman of the Month and was making more money than anyone in our office.

One day I asked Curtis to let me ride along with him during the day to see just what he did to be so successful. He let me go out with him for the day and it was at lunch that I learned a great lesson. When we finished eating, he got up, threw his trash away and was collecting himself to leave. I told him that we had another 40 minutes left for lunch and we could relax. He completely ignored me as he walked to the car.

I asked him if this was his daily routine. (Because it definitely wasn't mine. Mine was to extend lunch as long as possible.) His answer changed my life. Curtis was a sharp guy with a little stuttering problem. (I think he used his stuttering when needed!) He didn't stutter that day. He answered me with a question, *"Do you know another way?"* He said the only way he knew was to work hard and not waste time. What a mindset!

It is surprising that negative people, people who have not done the business or have done the business wrong, are always the ones who know the most about this industry. They will talk with you and attempt to give you advice from *THEIR* standpoint but it's all bad advice because they have failed to mention their laziness, or that they had a negative mindset, that they were not coachable, or that they neglected to do everything that was possible to make the business work. They just quit. That's why you want to do your GPM right away. And by all means, put your plan of action up where you can see it all the time. Keep in mind, the business is simple, but it is not easy. The business is not easy and it will get challenging. It's simple because there are only a few things you need to do on a consistent basis, but it's not easy because you are dealing with the human element, the melting pot of people; their different backgrounds, mindsets and nationalities.

Six Key Points

1. YOUR WHY: Why are you doing this? Paying bills is not a big enough "WHY." Your "WHY" must be strong enough so that when the challenges come along, and there will be plenty of them, you won't shut down. If your "WHY" isn't strong, you will forget what you spent, the sacrifices you've made and the time you set aside to get into the business.

You will unplug from the business and mentally shut the business down to take care of the small brushfires and the minor issues that seem so important at the time. When you finally walk away, there is no real sting. You really killed your business the moment you decided to unplug. You took yourself mentally out of the game when you unplugged and then you just walked around waiting to bury your business. But if your "WHY" is strong enough, it will lock you into your business, keep you in the business, create success in your business and keep you going in your business.

Most people are comfortable, meaning you have accepted having a couple of cars in the driveway, a couple of leather sofas throughout the house, a couple of flat screen TV's, and maybe a week's paid vacation once a year. If nothing ever changes in life, you are still comfortable. If your "WHY" is not strong enough, as long as you look the part, the image of what success looks like in America, if times get tough enough you can walk away from this business and still "look like" you are successful.

Most people in America feel that, *"It doesn't matter if I'm not doing good, if you think I'm doing good because I look the part, that's all that matters!"* But it's all a lie and you know it's a lie. And if your "WHY" isn't that strong, you'll settle for that lie. Some people...a lot of people even settle for the phrase, *"I'm working on some things, looking at some things and putting some things in place,"* which translates to, "I'm not doing anything but as long as you think I look like I'm doing something or I sound like I'm doing something, I'm great with that!" How long can a person live like that? Don't let this be you!!

When you are new in this business, _YOU MUST develop_ a strong enough "WHY." You have to continue to add bricks to your "WHY" to a point where a part time job or even over-time pay will not be satisfactory. It's sad and unfortunate that a lot of times the "WHY" is not taken seriously enough. The emphasis of it is not received the way it should be. What's really bad is many times it's completely overlooked.

From my years of experience, I must reemphasize that this probably is the most important step of your Game Plan Meeting. Developing your reason, developing your "WHY", developing the _unmitigated gall_ that you are not going to quit regardless of what comes up in your life and developing the audacity to continue to stay in the game through all the headaches, negativity, and nay-sayers until you climb that ladder and reach that pinnacle you're shooting for. This ought to be your declaration and your definitive stance!

You have to be determined that you will not stop until you reach your goal! You have to develop your "WHY," otherwise you are stopped before you start. Many times you lose out in business or you mentally leave the business before you ever develop that strong enough "WHY."

2. YOUR FINANCIAL GOALS: A.) What is your huge financial goal? Is it to make $200,000 a year? $500,000 a year? A Million a year? Now, I'm talking five to six years from now.

The other part to my question is: B.) When you start today, what is your goal a year from now? This in my eye-sight is very important. Because 12 months from now, if you don't have a financial goal that you're shooting for, you don't know if you're close, if you've hit it or if you're even in the ball park.

And I believe that in the first 12 months, it's so important to try to get close to what you're shooting for because that will give you the strength and the belief to continue in the business.

When you reevaluate your goals 12 months from now, have your goals changed? Will you be happy with the income that you have arrived at after 12 months? The income you have will only be from the work that you have put in up to that point.

You know and I know that it takes time, because anything in life worth getting will take time to get. My grandmother would always say, *"Baby, if you get it fast and quick, it ain't worth it!"* I know she wasn't talking about this business...we all know what she was talking about, but we can relate this analogy to what we are saying here because this is a get rich business but it is not a "get rich quick" type of business, even though many people want you to believe it is. It's crazy, but like I said before, the people that usually talk the most about the industry, know the most clichés, know the network marketing or the direct sales verbiage, have done the least amount of work and have made the smallest amount of money! How is that possible? And those are the ones who are quick to say that network marketing doesn't work.

Without discouraging them, I try to tell my new business partners, as well as people that I work with in general, the reality of this business when I'm talking with them. I want you to know the truth about the mental work, not physical work, that's really involved. If we can get our minds right and our thoughts right, then we can get our actions right. Then everything else will fall in place. This takes work.

The reason I say it's mental work is because, remember, we are dealing with the human element. We have a tendency to look at someone else's story and just think that we can cross over their same bridge without knowing the whole story of how they got across that bridge. We listen and mistakenly adopt their story as our own and think we can move as swiftly or as quickly as we *think* they have moved up through the company without realizing we have our own vein to follow.

We were not there at the *real* beginning of their chapter, we don't really know the whole, true story in the first place nor do we know what they brought to the table. We are on the outside looking in at the small bits of what they have told us. We only know the parts of what a person wants us to know. Is it possible to do it how they say they've done it? Maybe, but not probable because they had their road of experience to follow and we have our own.

When we're looking into someone else's fast track of success there is a possibility that we can get discouraged and throw in the towel after 12 months because a lot of times we get sidetracked and forget our 12 month goal by looking at what they're doing which in turn discourages us and then, *"BAM"* we are out of the game! You should never, ever try to follow someone else's road. You can admire people, you can listen and learn from them, but you still have to focus on your own road. Although this may sound like it's going against the six key points that I'm giving you, it's not, it's mindset. You don't want to set an unattainable goal for yourself by looking at someone else. You have to focus on your own road. That helps to build your *own* success story.

Here is an example of a typical conversation I might have in a GPM. Someone might say, *"I want to make $20,000 a month."* Which, I tell them is $240,000 a year and is of the top 4 to 5% of the money earners in the whole United States as of 2013.   *"That puts you among the top 18 million families! You can build up to that but it takes time. You set yourself up for failure if you expect to do that in just 12 months. It can be done. It has been done, but those are exceptions to the rule. And I would not build my business based on exceptions and examples based on someone else. Don't build your business based on someone else's example. Build it* *based on the reality of your own strength and build on that every day. And who knows, perhaps you will reach that. Don't set yourself up for that type of failure, especially inside the box of 12 months."* I get that type of huge expectation almost every time I do a GPM. After we have a detailed conversation, they come back down to reality. After we go over the Six Key Points, they understand more and then the ball is in their court.

You have to realize you can't always do what someone else can do. They may have the skills to do the extraordinary. You may have to be honest with yourself and accept that it will take time for you to gain the experience. Just keep in mind that it just takes time. It is a process. That extraordinary person that you're looking at has a different background than you and has taken the time to gain the experience. But once you have the experience, you have it! Then you have that experience that someone else will be looking to you to emulate. And the cycle continues. Then someone will look at you and wishing to be like you who have worked to gain experience and the cycles continues to build and duplicate.

3. YOUR SACRIFICE: Definition: Webster defines sacrifice as "a surrender of something for the sake of something else." It's very important in the beginning to know at least in the ball park what kind of sacrifices you are going to make. You might not know all of them because this is something new to you but you have to, at least, start off with a few sacrifices and get more precise as you go along. One thing is for sure, (you must know this which is sometimes shocking to people), you can't keep doing the same things or you'll continue to have the same results. I believe Webster defines that as insanity.

You're going to have to sacrifice some things that will cause a little pain because sacrifice should hurt. You're going from something that's not as important to something that is important. An example of that is one of my all-time favorite movies, The Untouchables Kevin Costner's character, Elliot

Ness, and Sean Connery's character, Jim Malone, are having a conversation about how to catch Al Capone, a big-time gangster. They were a Special Forces team put together by the government to go after Capone and his team of *bad* men and they were getting so very frustrated so they had to come up with a plan. Ness and Malone are sitting in a church after a funeral and they were highly upset. Malone says that the only way to catch this gangster is to think like a gangster and not like an agent, so he asks, "*Mr. Ness, What are you prepared to do? He pulls a knife, you pull a gun; He sends one of yours to the hospital, you send one of his to the morgue! That's the Chicago way. That's how you do that. Are you ready to do that? I just need to know. That's the only way we are going to stop him?*" So, I'm asking YOU, "WHAT are you willing to do? WHAT sacrifices are you willing to make?"

Also, there was an Olympiad who broke up with his girlfriend because he needed time to practice and concentrate on his performance. There's going to have to be a sacrifice to get what you want. You'll have to sacrifice things like: sleep, TV, food, friends, entertainment, hobbies, or things of that sort… something just for a moment to have a lifetime of what you want. When we say, "a moment," we don't know what that could be for you. One person's moment might be 6 months while another person's moment might be a year. But that has to happen in some form or fashion. That has to happen just for a moment in time to be comfortable for the rest of your life. You will do what you *have* to do, so that you can do what you *want* to do.

So always remember this when you are looking at the times that you are going to have to be uncomfortable and the times that you are going to have to work your business, 8am to 5pm pays your bills and pretty much keeps you average, keeps you ordinary, gets you by and keeps you mediocre, but 5pm to 1am is when you are going to change your life. And you are doing it consistently, mentally, physically and financially. That's how your life is going to become extraordinary!

And speaking of the Olympiad, during the time you are watching TV, you could be making phone calls, you could be listening to a business CD and you could be watching a business video or something to change your life. For most people, they are not willing to give up what entertains them. We deal with frustrations during the day and want to relax in the evening but remember, you voluntarily signed up in this business to change your life and to change yourself which means you are going to have to sacrifice and do some things that you don't normally do.

People choose this industry for the life and the fun, but they don't want to kiss the frog to get the prince, so-to-speak! As the story goes, the princess had to kiss the frog to get the prince, or the man of her dreams. In this case, you have to kiss the frog to get the life you desire or do something drastic to make the change happen in your life, but today people don't want to do that. What we are saying here is that there is no way around it, you're going to have to do drastic things to have drastic change. It might even seem that some people are getting lucky but trust me on this one, it all evens out in the end. You have to decide where *and* what you are going to sacrifice to get to where you are trying to go.

There's a friend of mine that's in the business with me that told me a story about his early frustration level in the business and how he started slacking off. He shared with me how he wasn't doing everything he was supposed to be doing. One day he looked up and months had gone by since he had done what he was supposed to do. He hadn't made any phone calls. He hadn't been to any meetings. He hadn't done any presentations. His wife didn't say anything, she just watched him and waited to see if he would get back to his business.

As they were sitting on the couch watching TV, disgusted with himself and his life, he turned to his wife and said, "Honey, promise me if I ever get into a vegetative state, you will pull the plug. I don't want you to sit and watch me exist until I die. Will you promise me that?" "Sure dear," she said. With that, she got up and pulled the TV plug out of the wall and said, "Now get back to that business, you promised us the world!"

Today, they have the lifestyle. They have the house. They have the cars. They go on many family vacations around the world, and they have the money. He sat down with his wife and reassessed his "WHY" for being in the business. He reestablished his goals and dreams and then went to working his business with a fire! He is a very successful network marketer, hitting the top of the company in four years!

You have to keep your desire in front of you. It's easy to get discouraged and fall back into your rut if you don't stay locked into your business every day. One day without business activity can easily grow into three days, then five days and before you know it, it's two months and so on. This is YOUR business and it's YOUR family and YOUR life that you are building this business for. Again, decide where you are going to sacrifice and what you are going to sacrifice. Make your plan. Stick to it and stick with it.

Some people are just not going to be able to cut it. You can't want it more for the people who you bring in. They have to want it for themselves. Never mind you can see how much of a success they can be. If they don't see themselves being a success, it just won't happen. The light bulb has to go off for them in their own head. You can't figure out the sacrifices for them, they have to do that. They have to see the need to sacrifice and move their life to a different level, and if they just don't see it, you have to move on and come back to them at another time. Like I said before, make your plan, stick to it and stick with it!

Whatever the sacrifice is, it's going to have to hurt to get what you want done. Only you can decide what that is and only you can make that happen. Let's say it's friendships. You may have friends that are not right for you. They weren't right for you from the start but you liked their quirky ways although you knew they were... *a little to the left.* You overlooked it because they made you laugh. Now that you are really going in a different direction, it matters. What do you do about the friendship? It's going to hurt but you will have to decide when and how to cut the relationship down and perhaps off.

People are either taking you to somewhere or pulling you away from somewhere. When you were young you didn't recognize it because you were growing up together, kind of going in the same direction, going to the same school, living in the same neighborhood and having the same experiences. When you began to develop your own sense of direction, you soon could see where they were pulling you or...where you pulling them. At some point a split has to occur if you are to grow and develop into the person you want to become. Otherwise you'll continue to just follow along with where they have been going and subsequently agreeing with their actions or opinions.

We all have heard the phrase, "Birds of

a feather flock together." It's true, in order for you to have friends, _real_ friends, you have to be in agreement. You have to agree with their life and their actions and a lot of their opinions for them to be your true friends. Here is something for you to think about: look at their life, look at their actions, and look at their opinions. Evaluate them and really see if you want to continue going that way. Look at whatever success they've had and assess if you want to continue going in the direction they are headed. If not, you are going to have to make some changes.

Once you get to where you are going, then you can reach back and invite them along if they are willing, that is, to join you. You are NOT in the business of pulling or dragging anybody with you. This is an individual journey that each of us has signed up for. And if sacrifices are not made, you will not have any success. Anything in life worth having is worth the sacrifice to get.

4. YOUR LIST: List Make a list of 100 names. This list is your collateral. This means you are serious. It is a known fact that if you are 18 years or older you know at least 1000 people by their first name. It is also a known fact that if you were preparing for a wedding or other large gathering that you'd be able to put your hands on at least half of those names and send them an invitation. Why? Because you want a gift! And we all know that half of those invited would not even respond or even show and that would not be a surprise. Half of all people invited to anywhere never show.

It's a struggle to get people to put those names on a sheet of paper. Many times we are adamant that we don't know that many people, but the real reason we don't want to put 100 names on our list is because we've already prejudged them.

We have all tried to guess or size folks up according to what we know or think about them. I did it too. In our mind we have already decided who will and who will not do this business. But how do we know that answer already? How do we know who has free flowing money and won't look at this industry? We don't know and what's sad is we won't give people a chance. We simply cancel people out by thinking we know their lifestyle. We are on the outside looking in. They might be hoping, looking and praying for an opportunity to change their life. How do we know unless we ask? The worst they could say is, *"No, I'm not interested."* So make that list and take time each day to add to your list. You add to it with the new people that you meet during your normal daily routine.

Some people's names you may not even know, but you know them by the experiences by which you've met them. For instance, the new guy that took your suit to be cleaned at the cleaners or the lady at the veterinarian's counter when you took Taffey in for her six-month shots.

You meet new people constantly so your list should grow constantly. Your list is your capital. That is the foundation of your business, and although we are in the electronic age and most people put their new prospect list in their phone, your list should not be left only in your phone. Certainly put the names in your phone, so that you can call and follow up with them quickly, but have those names written down just in case something devastating happens to your phone where you cannot get to your contact list. Some people are smart enough to have a backup system where they hook up their phone to their computer every so often and back up their information. You may do this but suppose you haven't gotten around to it this month and something happens to your phone? Your new names for your business are lost. Just get in the habit of writing the names in a notebook as well as your phone. Also it makes the business simple by putting it on a notepad. People are watching you and will try to copy what you are doing. It's easy to spend a $1.99 for a notepad and that can be duplicated.

5. YOUR LIST BY CATEGORIES: When you get your list written down, you want to place people in categories, by personality and then characteristics. These categories help you to remember the type of person that you've talked to or the type of person that you are going to talk to. The categories help you to remember how to talk to them and help you to tell your upline how to talk to them as well.

The first way to categorize your list is by personality:

- **REDS**: People that are doing very well and intimidate the heck out of you! Doctors, lawyers, coaches, and pastors, these are people you think are doing really well in their profession; People you look up to.

- **GREENS**: These people are your peers, they are equal to you. You partied together back in the day; you have the same car, same neighborhood, same job, same level of income, you've known them for most of your life.

- **BLUES**: These people look up to you. These people are easy to recruit because they do what you say, but they have no staying power. They will give you "the blues."

To get good results in your efforts of recruiting, you don't want all of any one color. You do want all of these colors. Here is my suggestion of the mix of how many of each color you should recruit:

You should recruit 1 RED, 10 GREENS and 20 BLUES to get the same successful results.

That one Red will have one in-home presentation at their house because they decided to do it. Remember, at their in-home presentation will be a lot of other Reds. Greens have a lot of contacts which is the majority of people we know. Blues will cause a lot of frustrations because they don't do much of anything and must be motivated to do everything. Remember, I told you they give you "the blues."

Don't go to a Blue because they really *need* it. Go to, and sign up a person because they really *want it* and *want to do this business.* That's what makes this business go is people who *want* this, not people who *need* this.

Usually what people are already doing outside the business is what people will be doing inside this business. For instance if they were successful and busy before they became part of the business, they will continue to be successful and busy and incorporate their new business into what they are doing but if you recruit Uncle Johnny just because he's sitting at home doing absolutely nothing, when you sign him up he will continue to do absolutely nothing.

Sign up people who *want* this as part of their life, not who need this as part of their life. If "need" were the case, the whole world would be here. Everybody needs better health, tax breaks, more money and whatever else your network marketing company provides but "want" is what's important here, not "need." That's what makes this business move and grow.

The second way to categorize your list is

by characteristic:

Not only will you categorize people by colors but you will also categorize them by a kind of fish. Yes, we use fish to help categorize as well.

URCHIN: They want to know all the facts.

WHALE: They want to help other people.

DOLPHIN: They want to have fun.

SHARK: They want to make money.

With those 100 names, categorize each name by color and then by fish. By doing so, it is easier to communicate with your upline when you do a 3-way call with them. You can now relay to the upline that the prospect is, for instance, a "Red Whale."

Don't go through the whole presentation with a prospect if he/she is a Shark. All they want to talk about is the money. Whales only want to talk about saving the world. Urchins want all the facts, literature, brochures, phone numbers, websites, etc. Dolphins only want to have fun. They don't care about the time of the event, they'll get there when they get there. They have never met a stranger; everyone is their friend.

You will encounter all of these types of people. Label everyone in your list so that you and your upline will know how to relate when you talk with them. If you are not relating to your prospect, you will lose them almost immediately. If you categorize your list, you can make it happen more smoothly. If all they want to talk about is the money, they will be very frustrated with you if you talk about helping people.

You will run across and want all of these kinds of people in your business. You have to know what language to use when talking with them. You have to relate to them otherwise you will lose them. You want to get to the point where you can listen for the clues, zero in quickly and speak their language in a limited amount of time. Ultimately, you want to build your business with a variety of categories of people because there are all kinds of people in the world. Having diverse business partners increases the potential for a worldwide business. The obvious being that it will appeal to more categories of people.

You want whales, many could be pastors, which will lead to their congregations hearing about this opportunity and signing up in YOUR business under the Pastor. You want Sharks who own their own businesses, which will lead to their business partners and friends hearing about this opportunity and signing up in YOUR business under your Shark business partner. You want Reds, who will lead to other Reds, who may be doctors, who may lead to their patients who might be lawyers and their lawyer friends and so on... You get my point.

I always get the question, "Do people have more than one personality?" Most people have maybe two of the three personalities and maybe two of the four characteristics. But you personally don't/can't have all of them. You are one dominant color and one dominant fish. For you to really have more than two of the characteristics and personalities you would have to be a diagnosed schizophrenic for them all to be really, really dominant. I've run across some people who are adamant about having all of the characteristics and all of the personalities. I am not making light of mental disorder, but you cannot have them all unless there is a mental imbalance. Some people, however will never be satisfied no matter what you say or do. Let them be who they say they are. You have a business to grow!

6. YOUR COMMITMENT: Commit to staying around for 12 months. After 12 months, if you stay in the game long enough, you are processing, reading, growing, emptying out your mental closet of old habits, filling your mind with new habits, listening to trainings, making your way to events and great things are happening to you. There is no way for you to be the same after 12 months. You begin to change. For some, the change starts to show in six months, and still for some it takes longer. But I guarantee you, if you stick with it, the change will come.

Let's look at a 16ft swimming pool vs. a

baby wading pool. Both are filled with dirty water and both represent two different types of people. The swimming pool has years of bad information, neglect, bad eating habits, bad schooling, real bad work ethic, etc... The baby wading pool is filled with the same thing, just a smaller version. These pools represent two different people who desperately want success to happen in their lives, who are both full of the same filthy water but in different proportions. It will take longer for one person to empty out of his bad experiences than for the other.

Where it will take one maybe one year, it may take the other maybe three years. But nonetheless, if they both stick it out, both of their pools of water will get cleaned out. Do you see my point here? It doesn't matter how long it takes, what matters is that if you have the fortitude to stick it out, it will happen for you!

You will get to the place in your development that you see yourself beginning to change and you like what you see but your old friends and old desires are still in you too. You know you can't go back, you can only go forward. You know that if you just keep going you'll change completely. You'll look different, talk different, and listen differently. The way you examine and process things will be different. Success will come for you if you want it and if you stay plugged in. And if you follow the system that's put in place by the leaders of the game, you know you will win.

You have to make a determination to keep moving forward no matter what. And when life hits, and it hits really hard sometimes, you have to already make up in your mind that you will figure out how to maneuver around the obstacles and keep moving forward.

Imagine if you had to get downtown to that court appointment and there was no way you could miss it, but without notice, there was construction on the freeway. You have no choice but to figure out how to get around that construction, whether it be side streets or the toll road which will take you out of your way. Even if you have to call someone else for another route, you will not miss that meeting with that judge especially if that means jail time! Once again, I hope you get my point! (I have to laugh at that one!)

The point is, you know many challenges are going to come up while you are on your journey so don't be surprised. Just go over it, under it, around it or in some cases burst right through it! Just get through life's situations and keep moving and don't quit!

The reason most people don't do the things that are suggested is because they don't believe in anything I have said. Maybe you think after 12 months, you should be at that great successful and financial goal. But reality says you have that 16 ft. pool full of dirty water when all along you thought it was just a baby wading pool. What does it matter? Just keep going. Can you really afford to stop now? Can you really afford to stop on your "WHY" and your "DREAMS" at this point? It takes time. To go from a dirty, mucky, dark pool to clear and clean water may take you

45

more time than you thought but the outcome might be more fantastic than you ever imagined. So what if it takes two or three years building this business while you work your job. Isn't two or three years going to pass anyway? You'll be a greater person for it in the end. You will have learned about the game of planning a strategy for building your network marketing business.

The Bible says, *"Call to me and I will answer you. I'll tell you marvelous and wondrous things that you could never figure out on your own."* Jer. 33:3 (Message Bible)

A year from now you may think you should be a lot further than you are, but if you are not doing these six steps and feeding these six steps to every person that comes into your business, your business will be filled with chaos. And not only that, if you are not building yourself up on the inside with reading books, listening to personal development CD's, hearing speakers, watching training videos and getting rid of empty information that does nothing to uplift your mind, you won't be any further than you are right now.

Someone asked me how many of my friends from my old circle are in business with me, my answer was simple, *"None! Their boat sank before they left the dock. They couldn't change their way of thinking. They didn't want to win bad enough. They thought they were okay working "ain't-to-faint," dark-30 to dark-30, 40 hours a week and waiting for the eagle to fly on Friday! I wanted more and I knew I could have it but I knew it was going to take work to get it. They didn't want to work for it. That's where we parted."*

Until you take the time to grow and build your "WHY" and work on yourself while you build and work these strategies of building your business, you will be wondering the same thing, "why?" Personal development, personal work and the strategies in the book go hand in hand.

As you change your thinking about your Network Marketing business, you will want to change your friends. You are going to want your friends to change their thinking too. If they can't or won't change, then you will have to change. In other words, *if you can't change your friends, change your friends!*

Your business has got to be of the utmost important thing in your life, right up there under God and then your family. Your business, if cared for in the right way, will help you care for your family better. So get that pool cleaned out and get a good understanding of these strategies and then teach them to each of your business partners one at a time and you will see your Game Plan working for you, I guarantee it. NOW you have a GAME PLAN!

Have a *FANTABULOUS* Day!

-Tony

Nuggets To Keep In Mind:

- You have to focus on your own road. That helps to build your own success story.

- Can you really afford to stop now? Can you really afford to stop on your "WHY" and your "DREAMS" at this point?

- The business is not easy and it will get challenging. It's simple, but not easy.

- If your "WHY" is not strong enough, as long as you look the part, if times get tough enough you can walk away from this business and still look like you are successful.

- Anything in life worth having is worth having to sacrifice to get.

- If you stick with it, the change will come.

- Usually what people are already doing outside the business is what people will be doing inside this business.

- People choose this industry for the life and the fun, but they don't want to kiss the frog!

- If you are not relating to your prospect, you will lose them almost immediately.

- My grandmother would always say, "Baby, if you get it fast and quick, it ain't worth it!"

- Having diverse business partners increases the potential for a worldwide business.

- I'm not doing anything but as long as you think I look like I'm doing something I'm great with that! How long can a person live like that? Don't let this be you!!

- You must have the fortitude to stick it

out no matter how long it takes.

- Categorize everyone on your list so that you and your upline will know how to relate when you talk with them. If you are not relating to your prospect, you will lose them almost immediately.

- A year from now you many think you should be a lot further than you are, but if you are not doing these six steps you won't be any further than you are right now.

- People have to know that it takes time. This is not a "get rich quick" type of business even though many people want you to believe it is. This is a get rich business, but not a get rich quick business.

- Build your business based on the reality of your own strengths and build on that every day.

- What are you willing to do? What sacrifices are you willing to make?

- 8am to 5pm is when you work your job. 5pm – 1am is when you change your life!!

- This is your business, your family and your life that you are building this business for.

- Make your plan. Stick to it and stick with it.

- This list is your collateral. This means you are serious.

- You meet new people constantly so your list should grow constantly.

- What makes this business grow is people who WANT this business, not the ones who NEED it.

- You should recruit 1 RED, 10 GREENS and 20 BLUES to get the same successful results.

- You have to make a determination to keep moving forward no matter what.

- If you can't change your friends, change your friends!

- I ask the big question, "What are you willing to sacrifice?"

- It's easy to get discouraged and fall back into your rut if you don't stay locked into your business every day.

- People are either taking you to somewhere or pulling you away from somewhere.

- You do begin to change if you don't quit.

- YOU MUST develop a strong enough "WHY" that can't be satisfied by a part-time job.

- Most of the time the answer for why your business hasn't taken off the way you want is right there in the mirror.

NOW, get started on your

GAME PLAN!

For more information on other books or training material, by Mr. Fleming or to schedule him for speaking engagements, please contact him at:
www.tonyflemingenterprises.com
Or you may send an email to:
mrtonyfleming@gmail.com

Upcoming Books From Mr. Fleming Include:

- *E.L.I.T.E.*
- *A Strong Enough Why*
- *You & Money*
- *The Sacrifice*
- *Make An "A" List*
- *Recruiter vs Builder*
- *24/7/365*
- *Basic System*
- *Becoming A "Message-Getter-Outter'er"*
- *You Gotta Love It*

The Game Plan

The Game Plan

The Game Plan

Made in the USA
Charleston, SC
11 August 2014